MANAGING CONSULTANCY

MANAGING CONSULTANCY

A Guide for Arts and Voluntary Organisations

Rick Rogers

National Council for Voluntary Organisations
and the Arts Council of Great Britain

Published by
National Council for Voluntary Organisations,
26 Bedford Square, London WC1B 3HU
and
Arts Council, 105 Piccadilly, London W1V 0AU

© NCVO/ARTS COUNCIL 1990

All rights reserved. No part of this publication may be reproduced or transmitted, in any form or by any means, electronic, mechanical, photocopying, recording or otherwise without the prior permission of the publishers.

British Library Cataloguing in Publication Data
Rogers, Rick
   Managing consultancy: a guide for arts and voluntary organisations.
   1. Great Britain. Voluntary organisations. Consultancy Services.
   I. National Council for Voluntary Organisations
   062

ISBN 0-7199-1295-4

Typeset by BookEns, Saffron Walden, Essex
Printed and bound in Great Britain by
J. W. Arrowsmith Ltd, Bristol

CONTENTS

Foreword   vii

Introduction   ix

What is consultancy?   1

Why use consultants?   7

Preparing for a consultancy   11
    Coping with change
    Handling disagreement
    Informing staff
    Involving staff
    Owning the consultancy

Preparing the initial brief   17

Finding consultants   21

Choosing the right consultants   25
    Preliminary discussions
    Interviewing the consultants
    What you should expect from the consultants

Agreeing the final brief with the consultants   31
    Timing and cost

What to do on appointment   37

Managing the consultancy 39
   When things go wrong
   The ethics of consultancy

Receiving the results 43

Assessing the outcome 45

After the consultancy 49
   Starting the debate
   Implementing the recommendations

Checklist for a consultancy 51

Where to find out more 55
   Organisations 55
   Publications 57
   References 59

FOREWORD

Arts and voluntary organisations are increasingly making use of consultants, usually to the satisfaction of all involved. Sometimes the experience is not rewarding and these instances are always disappointing. Working at the NCVO and the Arts Council has given us the opportunity to see consultancy commissions in progress and we talked together about the reasons for this disappointment.

Quite soon, we formed the view that the two main reasons, as far as the commissioning organisations were concerned, were lack of experience of the process and lack of confidence in their own judgement. The use of consultants is a comparatively new feature in the management of voluntary organisations and arts groups. It is not unreasonable to be unsure about an area where one's experience is limited.

Our decision to publish this book was based on our belief that, in providing a wider sharing of relevant experience, arts and voluntary organisations would benefit from the experience of their peers, be better equipped to start the process and, most importantly, be more confident in managing the consultancy.

Susan Elizabeth
National Council for Voluntary Organisations

Barry Jackson and Monica Tross
Arts Council of Great Britain

INTRODUCTION

This guide is designed to help you if you are considering using consultants or have already decided to do so but would like more information. It is based on interviews with arts and voluntary organisations which have employed consultants for a wide variety of purposes, with consultants who have carried out such work, and with funding bodies which advise organisations in the arts and voluntary sectors and provide schemes to help them gain more expertise in administrative, marketing, financial and other activities. It has also drawn on existing published material about consultancy work.

The arts and voluntary sectors are expanding their use of consultants as they seek to respond to the changes in the political, financial and social environment in which they have to operate – seeking new audiences; improving and redefining their services for existing and potential clients; exploring and becoming skilled in fresh activities; compiling a business or strategic plan; attracting new sources of income without compromising their basic or core values; meeting the demands of business with a response that is positive, businesslike and, above all, humane.

Consultants can help organisations do all these things –

along with more 'straightforward' tasks, such as assessing training needs or resolving internal differences. But it is vital that organisations first of all review their own capacity to undertake these tasks and, if they do decide to use outside help, that they go into such projects on equal terms with the consultants.

The aim of this book is to help arts and voluntary organisations decide whether to use a consultant and show how they can develop effective, enjoyable and equal partnerships with the consultants they employ. It advises on how to prepare for a consultancy and compile a detailed and accurate brief; find and choose the right consultants for the job; agree terms for carrying out a consultancy; manage the consultancy successfully; and what to do when the consultants report back.

WHAT IS CONSULTANCY?

Consultancy is nothing more nor less than advice and guidance. You are paying someone – an individual or a company, small or large – to give you detailed, intelligent, relevant and reliable advice on some issue of your organisation's work.

One book on management consultancy describes it as 'an advisory service contracted for and provided to organisations by specially trained and qualified persons who assist, in an objective and independent manner, the client organisation to identify management problems, analyse such problems, recommend solutions to these problems and help, when requested, in the implementation of solutions'.[1]

Consultancy requires two core ingredients – detailed knowledge of the field being looked at, and the ability to handle relationships successfully, or interpersonal skills. The latter are crucial in enabling consultants to win the trust of and to work with the people in an organisation – many of whom may be reluctant to confide in outsiders or suspicious of the consultancy.

Consultancy is neither training nor facilitating, although a

MANAGING CONSULTANCY

consultancy can contain elements of both – passing on skills and techniques, and helping people to change and develop, and reach solutions among themselves. Nor is it managing, which is quite a different skill. A manager is a doer; a consultant thinks and reflects and helps others to do so, working through a joint process of bringing about change.

Consultants come in three basic types – individual freelance consultant, the small-scale consultancy, and the large city-based accountancy company which offers consultancy services. Many of these companies are expanding into the arts and voluntary sectors. The individual, freestanding consultant and the small-scale consultancies tend to be people who have moved over to consulting from careers in the arts or voluntary sectors.

Consultants can provide specific technical expertise over a short period, such as advising on a computer system for the organisation, assessing training needs, setting up new box-office arrangements; work with an organisation over a longer time-span on, for example, a strategic plan, re-organising and encouraging greater involvement in decision-making processes; or move in and out of an organisation intermittently as and when it needs advice.

Both arts and voluntary organisations are making increasing use of consultants as they seek to respond to shifts in the social and artistic demands being made on them and the changing financial and political enviroment in which they must, or wish to, operate – looking to adapt their aims, sources of income, organisation or staffing structure to be better able to cope with and make the most of such changes.

Examples of the tasks entrusted to consultants by arts and voluntary organisations include helping to:

▶ identify and win new sources of funding;
▶ change work practices;

WHAT IS CONSULTANCY?

- plan better support for local branches;
- move premises;
- devise a three-year development plan;
- resolve tensions, differences, and interpersonal conflicts within an organisation.

Consultants can work in different ways. For example, some people divide them into 'experts' and 'collaborators' – those who operate as 'technicians', coming into an organisation, identifying the problem, offering a solution, and moving on – disturbing the organisation as little as possible; and those who are more collaborative in their approach, working with an organisation and its staff and exploring and seeking solutions together. Needless to say, such definitions are exaggerated, with most consultants a mix of the two approaches.

They can be employed for different reasons. A recent NCVO series of meetings on consultancy work produced a list of roles that organisations gave the consultants they hired, including: someone to validate unpopular decisions, someone to perform a holding or stabilising function, the expert, the facilitator, the hit-squad (recommending something unpleasant the organisation is unable to do itself), and the catalyst for change.

By and large, the voluntary sector is further along the track of consultancy work and experience than the arts sector. 'Management and the language of management, marketing and business have come to the arts world later than in the voluntary sector because the latter have had to live on their wits for longer,' commented one consultant.

But the last five years have seen a major sea-change in both sectors as organisations strive to come to terms with this area of expertise and seek to win new opportunities from it.

There has been a growth in the number and type of consultants seeking business in these sectors. The Arts Council

3

has details of over 300 consultancies dealing with the arts sector. The National Council for Voluntary Organisations knows of over 200 consultancies already working with the voluntary sector. The major accountancy companies have created special departments to handle such business, under such headings as 'leisure and tourism' or 'public sector'. Small-scale consultancies or individual consultants have been set up by people coming out of arts and voluntary organisations.

Much of the arts world has been taken up with marketing reviews and what one arts administrator called the 'short-sharp-blitz consultancy', such as finding a new name for the organisation or reviewing publications policy. But these must now be set alongside the growth of more fundamental and long-term projects such as developing management structures and helping organisations acquire expertise rather than providing it as an arm's-length service – leaving the organisation largely untutored in carrying out such services themselves. Another trend is away from analysing internal operations towards setting out the strategic direction of the arts in a region, integrating it with other sectors, and making a public case for arts development.

The voluntary sector is already well along the path of major reviews of activities and structures, together with enhancing staff development and training to enable them to take advantage of new areas of income-generation and become more enterprising and effective. The potential, and actual, clash between ends and means is a lively debate in the voluntary sector. For example:

> 'We need to link together concerns about what we are doing philosophically with such activities as marketing and strategic planning to ensure we are sustainable.'

> 'The real challenge for voluntary sector organisations may lie in adopting from the commercial world where it has skills which can genuinely help the organisation to meet the changes it faces, be these planning

WHAT IS CONSULTANCY?

processes, marketing or accountancy, but not to lose its value base in the process.'

Many arts and voluntary organisations are taking on consultants, developing successful working partnerships and getting good results that do not endanger core-values. This highlights that, handled knowledgeably and with confidence, consultants need not be viewed as trojan horses but rather as valuable allies in an inevitable process of change.

How the Institute of Management Consultants defines Consultancy

A management consultant is an independent and qualified person who provides a professional service to business, public and other undertakings by:
(1) identifying and investigating problems concerned with strategy, policy, markets, organisation, procedures and methods;
(2) formulating recommendations for appropriate action by factual investigation and analysis with due regard for broader management and business implications;
(3) discussing and agreeing with the client the most appropriate course of action;
(4) providing assistance where required by the client to implement his/her recommendations.

WHY USE CONSULTANTS?

'Having an outsider in provoked change – and change is very difficult in any organisation, especially a long-established one like ours. We recognised we had to change but we didn't know how.'

That comment is from a voluntary-sector administrator who had mixed feelings about the outcome of an in-depth assessment of his organisation by a firm of management consultants. There were problems of detail, but the basic value of bringing in a consultant was never doubted.

Organisations use consultants when they can gain some benefit from doing so. This simplistic statement is the one common factor in a wide spread of specific reasons for bringing in consultants.

Consultants should be able to provide an organisation with something it has not got – be it expertise, extra time, an outside view, the ability to ask questions that cannot be asked by an insider, the skills to solve a problem proving intractable. They can perform tasks that the organisation, for one reason or another, cannot do itself. An organisation should expect to be different in some way after the consultancy.

Nevertheless, organisations need to think carefully before taking on consultants to do a job they may well be able to do themselves, or where they feel that it is as important for the organisation to go through the process of planning itself as it is to come up with a solution. Some consultants will be able to assist such a process, others not, preferring to work more at arms' length.

Indeed, one view is that consultants should be able to do nothing that cannot be done internally – except provide an outside view or external validation for a course of action – if only an organisation had the time, specialist expertise, or sufficient staffing.

'There must be the capacity within an organisation to implement the recommendations made; therefore the capacity should also exist to formulate what needs to be implemented,' suggested one arts administrator. What consultants can do that organisations cannot, she argued, is to be good facilitators, and to ask difficult or the 'right' questions. For example:

> 'In the process of strategic planning they can be of crucial assistance, if properly used. They can be agents for speeding up and easing the process. They can ask hard questions which people in an organisation may find difficult to ask, or may never have formulated "because we've always done things like that". They can uncover tensions between staff and board, or within each, and can manage these tensions constructively and creatively. They can focus and assist the process of planning. It is not a good idea to have them perform the process for you.' [2]

Other reasons cited include buying in 'clout' on the assumption that decisionmakers will take more notice of an outside expert's view than an inhouse one, and buying in skills – 'the process of transferring skills, experience and even structures, relating to such areas as personnel, marketing, or finance'.

WHY USE CONSULTAI

Some organisations turn to consultants through a lacl self-confidence, under-estimating their own ability to deal effectively with problems and dilemmas. The same failing can affect organisations when they decide that calling in consultants *is* a valuable exercise, but still feel the weaker party rather than an equal or controlling partner.

One consultant explained: 'There is a tendency to use consultants too much and not intelligently enough. The way to use them is to say: here is something we haven't done before, let's get a consultant to take us through this, so we can do it ourselves next time. That way you are not deskilling your own organisation.' Thus the knack is to use consultancy in a way that enhances the organisation rather than damaging it through lowering morale or making staff question their own competence.

So you think you need consultants

▲ are their skills really necessary?
▲ what extra dimension would they add?
▲ what are the expected benefits over doing the work inhouse?
▲ are the benefits likely to be worth the extra cost?
▲ could bringing them in create any special problems?
▲ are there longer term benefits or risks?[3]

PREPARING FOR A CONSULTANCY

Bringing consultants in can have a profound effect on an organisation and those who work for it. Therefore it is vital that everyone knows consultants are coming in and is adequately prepared for them. There are two elements to contend with – the fact of the consultancy, and the changes that it will inevitably generate.

COPING WITH CHANGE

The decision to take on a consultancy suggests that the organisation is willing to make changes – for example, to the way it is run, to the people who work for it, to the services it offers and the people it serves, to the funding it receives and from where. That decision is a first step, but it ought to be seen as one that could well mean major changes, which will certainly bring extra work in the short term, new tensions, and fresh opportunities, and some hard decisions. While the thought of change can be exhilarating, the act of change often causes problems. So it is worth asking the following questions: Is the organisation capable of change? Are those who work for it willing to consider the possibility of, and potential for, change?

HANDLING DISAGREEMENT

Any disagreements within an organisation about the proposed consultancy can, and should, be resolved before the consultancy starts – for example, whether to employ outside consultants at all, the budget for the work, who gets to talk to the consultants, who should sit on any steering group, and so on. If such aspects are not sorted out in advance, you may find you are paying the consultants to sort them out for you or will be wasting their time and your money if these unresolved issues impede the progress of the consultancy work.

However, if disagreements relate specifically to the issue being analysed by the consultants, such as the current or future direction of the organisation, its programme, its funding sources, then such matters are relevant to the consultants and they should be enabled to listen to them and assess them as part of their work. Indeed, one could argue that the first kind of disagreements fall into this category too if the organisation is incapable of sorting them out.

There should be few problems if the proposed consultancy is straightforward, such as deciding on the most appropriate computer system. Not so easy, perhaps, if the issue is a controversial one, such as a major structural change, responding to a financial crisis, or seeking a change of direction. The latter call for careful and sensitive preparation.

INFORMING STAFF

All those who work for the organisation should therefore know about the consultancy and why it is to take place. Make sure everyone is clear about what the consultants are to be asked to do: what the problem or issue is; why it exists; what the advantages are of bringing in someone from outside; what we want the consultancy to do for us.

PREPARING FOR A CONSULTANCY

The co-operation and, if possible, support of staff is a vital element in a successful outcome. This becomes even more important if a consultancy has been 'imposed' on the organisation – say, by its management board or committee, or major funder.

Three key questions to consider are:

▶ How might the consultancy affect people's own working situation (at least temporarily) and what might be demanded of them, such as providing information, taking on extra work, and talking to the consultants?
▶ In what ways will staff (and which staff) be involved in the consultancy – directly and indirectly?
▶ What sort of difficulties and tensions might arise within the organisation because of the presence of consultants and what they are looking at?

The way you tackle these issues obviously depends on the kind of organisation you are, who has commissioned the consultants in the first place, and what they have been brought in to make recommendations on. But the desired outcomes are the same – consultants who receive the co-operation, information and insights they need to produce a valuable report; and staff who respond confidently to the presence of, questioning by and demands of the consultants.

INVOLVING STAFF

Some people will be more involved and more directly affected than others. Decide:

▶ whether to set up a steering group that represents and can articulate the interests of and ideas from all groups or members of staff – bearing in mind that such an arrangement must not become cumbersome or unbusinesslike, needlessly hampering the con-

sultancy and developing as an ineffective vehicle for expressing ideas and concerns;
▶ who will help in preparing and agreeing the brief; how the consultants will be chosen and who will be involved in that process;
▶ whom to appoint to act as the main contact for the consultants;
▶ how staff will be kept in touch with the progress of the consultancy – this can be a crucial element in a successful consultancy and a common difficulty for an organisation in need of an outside assessment of its work and the way it operates;
▶ how to report back to staff when the consultancy has been completed – this may well depend on what comes out of the consultancy and the details of reporting back will have to be agreed later.

OWNING THE CONSULTANCY

'You have to feel that the problem is yours if you are going to engage and work with a consultant. Many consultancy relationships fail because the client does not feel "ownership" of the problem.'[3]

Some organisations report that a consultancy was something done to them rather than something they felt an integral part of. They felt the consultancy wasn't theirs; they didn't 'own' it. The notion of 'owning' a consultancy can mean two things:
▶ enabling the people who work in an organisation to feel in control of a consultancy and to regard it as 'their' consultancy, thereby generating a positive approach rather than a neutral or negative one.
▶ ensuring that they also feel they remain responsible for the 'problem' once the consultants have started work.

Uncertainty about owning a consultancy can happen when organisations fall into the trap of handing their problem

PREPARING FOR A CONSULTANCY

over to the consultants and making it the consultants' problem rather than theirs. Another cause of uncertainty can be when the consultancy is imposed from above – that is, from a board of managers or trustees, a funding body, or an individual decision by a director or general secretary.

'Don't just see it as a convenient way of parking your problem elsewhere for a while . . . it's worth remembering that the key to a successful client/consultant relationship hinges on the extent to which responsibility for any proposed activity is jointly held.'[4]
In effect: It's your project; maintain ownership.

Consultancy offers many rewards for an organisation. But it is no easy option – either to solving a problem, making improvements, or developing a new strategy. Preparing properly can make all the difference between a successful and a disappointing consultancy.

- ▲ Discuss the proposed consultancy in the organisation and how people are likely to be involved in and affected by it.
- ▲ Make sure everyone is clear about what the consultancy is about, the advantages of bringing in consultants, and what they are expected to do.

Decide:
- ▲ whether to set up a steering group;
- ▲ who will prepare and agree the brief;
- ▲ how to choose the consultants;
- ▲ who will be the main contact for the consultants;
- ▲ how the organisation will be kept in touch with
- ▲ the progress of the consultancy.

PREPARING THE INITIAL BRIEF

Getting the brief right is at the heart of a successful consultancy. Preparing an initial brief in advance of finding a consultant requires a good deal of time and effort. But such an exercise can usefully:

- focus the organisation's attention on the task ahead,
- give reality to any proposed consultancy,
- draw in or from a wide range of people working for
- the organisation (encouraging 'ownership' again),
- help to clarify the issues facing the organisation.

For example, if it is a 'negative' issue – such as a financial crisis – a brief can set that in the context of a more 'positive' search for a new role. If it is a desire to expand operations or services, then the brief can provide a coherent and realistic framework.

Many organisations set out to produce a brief by forming a planning or working group. This can be useful for consultants who are to carry out a major assessment of an organisation; less so for those carrying out more straightforward tasks, such as advising on computer needs or a public relations strategy.

It is as well to start by setting down the organisation's

overall aims or mission statement. 'Without aims, it is impossible to decide on the means . . . If an organisation does not know what it wants to achieve it cannot check if it is doing it.'[5]

The initial brief should identify the issue/problem; suggest how to carry out the work; set out the values of the organisation; define aims of the consultancy – 'where do we want to be afterwards?'; propose an initial budget and time-scale.

In the end, though, the basic or core brief can be quite short. For example:

To propose an effective organisational structure and associated procedures for the management and support of XYZ's regional offices; and to develop the central office structure to take into account proposed changes in the regional structure and other structural inadequacies currently experienced.

or

Carry out a feasibility study to set up a trading company.

or

Review the organisation's printed material and recommend a publications policy.

This is an important stage during which an organisation should clarify as far as possible what it wants the consultants to do and where it wants to be at the end of the consultancy. This is not to say the brief, once put together, should be set in stone. Rather that it should be full enough to be changed at agreed steps through the processes of choosing and negotiating with consultants, and of working through the consultancy itself. So it might be useful to build into the timetable, points at which the brief should be reviewed if necessary – such as after discussing the consultants' proposal in the light of the brief.

PREPARING THE INITIAL BRIEF

Consultants often report that the decisionmakers in many arts and voluntary organisations are unclear about what they want to come out of a consultancy. One consultant commented: 'Briefs are often a long way from what can be delivered. They need to focus on the realities rather than the dreams.' In return, many consultants are themselves ambivalent about their role in relation to the arts and voluntary sectors: for example, are they experts or facilitators of the expertise of others? Indeed, one consultant avoids using the word as much as possible, preferring what she regards as the more informative 'guidance' or 'advice'.

Much of this is due to a mutual lack of familiarity. But it is a gap that is rapidly closing as both sides see more the advantages of working together and become more knowledgeable about each other.

Suffice to say that presenting consultants with a detailed brief with clear, workable objectives will show you mean business and are being businesslike. There will be no danger that any consultants will do other than take you seriously.

The initial brief should:
- ▲ identify the issue/problem;
- ▲ suggest how to carry out the work;
- ▲ set out the values of the organisation;
- ▲ define aims of the consultancy – 'where do we want to be afterwards?';
- ▲ propose an initial budget and time-scale.

FINDING CONSULTANTS

There are three main ways of finding consultants and asking them to tender for the job - by personal recommendation (word-of-mouth), by seeking advice from organisations that monitor the consultancy world, or by advertising.

Word-of-mouth

This can be a valuable, time-saving way of identifying suitable consultants. Talking informally with like-organisations which have had experience of particular companies or individual consultants working on similar issues or problems to your own. This method can throw up a quick shortlist of candidates to be questioned more closely about their suitability for *your* organisation.

Word-of-mouth can work well when you know and trust those who advise you and who share a similar culture and set of values. But it can also restrict your choice if you are not made aware of new consultants, or if the other organisations made their choice from a limited pool of candidates. You should check that those advising you had the same kind of concerns and imperatives as you in choosing. For example, the need for specific specialisms, the importance of a balance of gender, race, or sexual orientation in the consultancy team or experience of the issues involved.

Consultant-watchers

A range of organisations now offer lists, databases, and advice on individual consultants and companies across the various fields, such as marketing, management, training, computers, fundraising, and so on. The services offered can extend from providing lists to acting as 'brokers' in matching organisation to consultant (see below).

Advertising

This can be a way to get the most competitive price for the job, and to ensure fairness, not so much for the consultants but rather to avoid bias in an organisation's choice – choosing only what you are familiar with rather than what you may actually need. However, advertising is not a foolproof method of ensuring equal opportunity nor of getting the most appropriate consultant for your task. It should therefore be used flexibly. For example, allow the case to be made for not going out to tender or for not accepting the lowest price if other factors should take precedence.

Where to find consultants

The Arts Council Marketing Department offers advice linked, in part, to its database of marketing and management consultants, which includes full details of over 300 companies and individuals – services offered, experience, specialisms, fee rates, and so on. The Arts Council also offers training opportunities and general advice on organisational development. **Contact** The Arts Council, 105 Piccadilly, London W1V OAU; phone 071 629 9495.

The National Council for Voluntary Organisations (NCVO) Management Unit offers several services to voluntary organisations, including a brokerage service which brings together suitable consultants and organisations, supports organisations through the contracting process, and monitors the consultancy work as it progresses on behalf of the voluntary organisation. Alongside the brokerage function,

FINDING CONSULTANTS

the Unit supports a network of consultants, encouraging the development of knowledge and skills appropriate for working with the voluntary sector and meeting its consultancy needs. In addition, the NCVO's Organisational Development Unit can offer advice on ethnic minority issues and concerns in relation to consultancy work. **Contact National Council for Voluntary Organisations, 26 Bedford Square, London WC1B 3HU; phone 071 636 4066.**

Other sources include:

▶ Chartered Institute of Marketing, Moor Hall, Cookham, Berkshire; phone 06285 24922.
▶ Institute of Charity Fundraising Managers, 208 Market Towers, Nine Elms Lane, London SW8 5NQ; phone 071 627 3436.
▶ London Voluntary Service Council, 68 Chalton Street, London NW1 1JR; phone 071 388 0241.
▶ Museums & Galleries Commission, 7 St James's Square, London SW1Y 4JU; phone 071 839 9341.
▶ National Institute for Social Work, Mary Ward House, Tavistock Place, London WC1H 9SS; phone 071 387 9681.
▶ your regional arts association, area museum council, local council for voluntary service, or voluntary sector coordinating group.

CHOOSING THE RIGHT CONSULTANTS

There are five basic stages to choosing the consultants for the job: drawing up a list of likely consultants; finding out more about them; assessing their proposals for doing the job; interviewing a shortlist of candidates; and making the final selection.

First, compile a criteria checklist for shortlisting consultants, involving the most important elements you are looking for, such as track record in similar jobs, awareness of special needs of target groups, high level of consultation with client, ability to undertake the work in the given timescale and the given budget.

Give those consultants on your 'likely' list details of the organisation, the reasons for calling in consultants, and a copy of your initial brief. Make it clear that you are approaching other consultants at the same time (if you are).

Draw up a list of consultants to speak to. It is advisable to interview in detail only two or three different consultants. You may want to talk initially to a larger number and then draw up an interview-shortlist (see Preliminary discussions), or go straight to detailed discussions with a smaller number (see Meeting the consultants).

PRELIMINARY DISCUSSIONS

Once you have a shortlist of candidates, start preliminary discussions with them – and within your own organisation. Confirm that any first-time meeting and work done on submitting a proposal based on your initial brief will not be charged for.

Check with the consultants:

- Are they really interested in the work?
- Have they done similar work – if so, with whom?
- Do they have the specialisms you may need?
- What do they charge?
- When will they be available to take on your project?
- Who will actually be doing the work?
- Do they appreciate your organisation's culture and set of values? ('Could we work together?')

Assessing the last point is a matter of listening to the answers they give and the language they use, the questions they ask – and the ones they don't. Do they understand that different organisations can have different cultures and ways of working? They don't have to work the way you do, but they should be happy about working with you. A crucial deciding factor could be: do you like them?

Ask not more than three of the consultants in whom you are most interested to submit a proposal for the job to include:

- its aims and objectives;
- how they propose to carry out the job (eg interviews, questionnaires, etc);
- where feasible an estimate of fees, expenses and likely timescale on the basis of the information you have provided so far;
- some background on the consultants themselves.

Some consultants may prefer to meet you first before submitting a detailed proposal.

Give the shortlisted consultants the opportunity to find out more about your organisation so that they can come up with good ideas about how to go forward.

Check out any references provided by the consultants – and with those organisations you know they have worked for but are not given as referees. A less-than-successful consultancy elsewhere shouldn't by any means rule someone out – it may not have been the consultants' fault, but it is worth knowing the full story – and how a company or individual handled a difficult project may provide valuable insight into how they may work with you.

Finalise the arrangements within the organisation for choosing the consultants to do the job. Circulate details of the shortlisted candidates to all appropriate people in the organisation.

INTERVIEWING THE CONSULTANTS

Make sure you are interviewing the person/people who will actually carry out the work for you or who is to be your principal contact within the consultancy firm. Go through their proposal and your brief together.

At the meeting, consider the following points:

- ▶ do they show an understanding or your problems and/or the issues involved?
- ▶ do they listen to what you say and amend and rethink accordingly?
- ▶ do they appear competent and experienced?
- ▶ do you like them and feel comfortable with them?
- ▶ are they offering tailor-made solutions or do they accept that each job is different – if not wholly different?
- ▶ do they show an appreciation of or sympathy for the culture and values of your organisation?
- ▶ will they also be sufficiently objective or hardheaded to offer recommendations and ideas that may be

MANAGING CONSULTANCY

   painful or unpleasant, but nonetheless demand consideration; and sufficiently sensitive not to offer 'impossible' solutions that go against the organisation's core-values?
▶   do they reveal an understanding and commitment to equal opportunities, implicitly and explicitly, in discussing the way the job should be carried out and the proposed outcomes?
▶   do they challenge elements of the brief or the way you perceive the job being carried out? (Wholehearted agreement suggests they have not thought the issues through. Remember that you won't have a perfect brief nor complete understanding of what you need.)

You need to discuss:

▶   who will do the work and how many people will be working on your job;
▶   the consultants' experience with your kind of organisation and the issues involved – discussing both successes and difficulties;
▶   the schedule for the job – how much time the job requires and over what sort of period it can be carried out;
▶   arrangements for monitoring, reporting back and opportunities for reassessment during the work;
▶   the fee and how it will be paid;
▶   the estimated costs involved (including expenses and VAT), how they break down, and how expenses will be controlled;
▶   whether payments should relate to completing specific stages of the job.

After you have interviewed all the candidates:

▶   eliminate those not suitable;
▶   compare the strengths and weaknesses of the rest;
▶   compare the fees quoted and the estimated timescales, including the number of days;
▶   check on points that need clarification;

CHOOSING THE RIGHT CONSULTANTS

▶ assess genuine enthusiasm (as opposed to a sales pitch) and level of constructive ideas (even though you may not have agreed with some of them).

How do you choose? It is likely to be a mix of their expertise and credibility, and your commonsense. Look at value for money, the 'right' commitment and set of values, appropriate experience, being well recommended by people you trust. All these will play a part. You may well have to balance advantages and disadvantages – for example, getting the timing right for carrying out a consultancy can be more important than accepting the least expensive proposal. But an over-riding factor is: do you get on well with them?

What you should expect from the consultants

▲ to identify and explain fully the perceived problems/opportunities/issues based on first-hand observation and analysis of your organisation;
▲ to recommend objectives that meet your needs;
▲ to advise on the consequences and cost of the recommendations made and how to implement them;
▲ to give evidence to back their recommendations and to help you come up with your own answers;
▲ to produce recommendations as a final written report and/or in any other form agreed as most appropriate for your needs;
▲ to be willing to negotiate some form of follow-up meeting after the delivery of the final report.

AGREEING THE FINAL BRIEF WITH THE CONSULTANTS

Discuss your initial brief with the consultants on the basis of 'this is what we think we need'. Unless you are sure that it reflects what you want, treat the initial brief as a negotiating document or tool during the setting up of a consultancy. Once agreed, treat the final brief as a reference point throughout the consultancy. It should set out what you expect the consultants to deliver.

In addition, and if appropriate to the proposed work, divide the brief into stages, with each stage being assessed before deciding whether and how to go ahead with the next stage. There are several reasons for this:

▶ The best consultancies are a dynamic partnership rather than static – the process of asking and being asked questions about why you do what you do, especially by people from outside an organisation, can create fresh insights and open new avenues to investigate which should be written into the brief.
▶ Refining the brief together enables the consultants to learn about the organisation and what makes it tick. One voluntary organisation director commented: 'There is the danger of a consultant who doesn't know the culture of an organisation and making wrong assumptions. No two organisations are alike.'

MANAGING CONSULTANCY

- ▶ Negotiating the brief also allows the organisation to draw on the experience of the consultant in refining the framework or parameters of the consultancy. This also enables the concept of a partnership to be developed from the beginning.
- ▶ In turn, some consultants do not like very detailed, rigid briefs. 'They often ask the wrong questions,' commented one consultant. 'Sometimes the problem for the consultant is not to find an answer but to ask the right questions.' In effect, what can happen is that an organisation knows where it wants to get to, but isn't clear on how best to do so.
- ▶ 'The brief is often not a good indication of what people really want,' said another consultant. 'We need to go and talk to them to get a feel for what is going on behind the brief. Then we can tell whether we are in tune with who they are and what they want to do; whether they are on the right track – and if on the wrong one, assessing if they are prepared to change to a different one.'
- ▶ Consultants also like to build new steps into a brief. For example, one insists on initial confidential sessions with all the staff of an organisation in order to establish a trusting relationship with them.

You may wish to refine the brief in two ways:

- ▶ matching it with how shortlisted consultants respond to it in their tendered proposal and preliminary discussions (which you would not expect to be billed for);
- ▶ and/or working with the favoured consultants before the actual consultancy begins to finalise a mutually agreeable document. This may be treated as separately contracted, billable work taking not more than a day.

The latter method has additional advantages – over and above having settled on a final brief:

- ▶ each gets a taste of working with the other;

AGREEING THE FINAL BRIEF WITH THE CONSULTANTS

▶   last-minute difficulties can be identified and resolved outside the actual consultancy;
▶   if things don't work well, each side can withdraw from or seek to amend the proposed consultancy.

In treating the brief as a negotiating tool, you have a better chance of ending up with a tool that will do the right job for you. One danger is that it will be refined more to suit the consultants' needs than yours – swinging it towards a project that is less demanding for them or for which they have an off-the-shelf 'solution'. The danger can be reduced by being aware of such a response during the selection process; by being confident about the basic thrust of your brief and not being afraid to ask questions. Be assertive and expect them to justify any major changes. For example, one recent survey of consultancy work found that:

> 'Client pressure is driving most of the changes taking place in consultancy. For instance, a well-worn allegation about management consultants in the 1970s was that they adopted a "cookie-cutter" approach: they redefined the brief to match their preconceptions, and they prescribed solutions based on whatever prefabricated model had been the flavour-of-the-month when they were in business school. Nowadays, clients are more assertive about what they think consultants should be studying.'[6]

TIMING AND COST

Two crucial questions in preparing any brief are: how long should the consultancy take, and how much will it cost?

The timescale of a consultancy might be easy to agree: you may just want to 'buy' a specific amount of time – a day's work to discuss training needs or a week to assess computer needs. But how long does it take to devise a new strategic plan or re-organise the financial basis of an organisation?

MANAGING CONSULTANCY

Again, make your own estimate and then compare consultants' assessments. Ask about the differences and decide which seems most reasonable. Don't go automatically for the one offering the shortest time-scale. It is important to allocate the right amount of time to do the job properly.

One option is to agree stages in the timetable at which timing and cost can be regularly assessed and, where necessary, revised. Often getting the timing right is more important than meeting the most economical costing.

'Organisations are not very good at assessing cost,' claimed one consultant, but acknowledging, 'it is very difficult because of the tremendous range of prices charged by different kinds of consultant.' Another commented: 'Some organisations think it is a lot of money for a few days' work; they are just not familiar with the rates.' And one arts organisation director's first comment when asked about the impact of a consultancy: 'It was a lot of money!'

One organisation offered a fee of £5,000 for a project over 8 weeks to carry out research and promotional work because that was what was left in the relevant budget heading; another offered £8,000 for a consultancy on job descriptions and a strategic plan because that is what they thought the job was worth. Both had a significant response.

A first step can be to find out a range of consultancy charges and fix an initial budget based on how many days of the consultants' time the job should take. This should give you a starting-figure to bounce off interested consultants.

Reaching a final figure means acquiring proper estimates based on the brief from a range of companies and individual consultants and matching these to the suitability of those consultants and the starting-figure budget.

Does your brief require 'the resources, specialisms and methodology of a big company' or 'the specific, well-

AGREEING THE FINAL BRIEF WITH THE CONSULTANTS

honed expertise of a small consultancy or individual'? The key question is, which is right for you? Your particular kind of specialism may exist within a large or a small company; an individual consultant may have specialised in what you need. If you're big you may think you need a big consultancy, but it depends more on the job you want done. A big job can fall within the remit of a small consultancy. Check with like-organisations what sort of consultancy they employed for a similar job to yours.

Compare the fees quoted and how they are calculated: a fixed fee or daily rate? Overall, there are two main financial arrangements: a set fee for a set task, and billable hours – daily rates billed at the end of each month. A fixed fee is generally better for a one-off project; a daily rate for an open-ended agreement for guidance as and when required.

Check how closely your budget matches the fee quoted in relation to your brief. It is essential to indicate in your brief what your budget is – some consultancies will adjust their proposal and fee to match the budget and still meet the brief satisfactorily. One consultant said: 'Costing a job can be "strategic" and flexible depending on whether you have a lot of spare people at the time and you are in need of a project, you want to get the organisation on your books, or you want to break into a particular sector.'

The professional bodies representing consultants offer a range of advice and standards of professional behaviour for agreeing payment for consultancy work. One regards it as 'unprofessional conduct' to agree payment 'on any basis other than a fixed fee agreed in advance'; another says only that fees will 'be based on service provided on specific task carried out'.

So reach agreement on a basis for charging and how it will be paid, for example, by initial and final instalment, or monthly with a fixed limit, which is most suitable for you. As one consultant remarked: 'In the end, we want a happy client who feels they have got value for money.'

The Institute of Management Consultants[7] offers the following guidance:

There must be a clear understanding between client and consultant:

- ▲ as to the objective of the assignment;
- ▲ the fees or the basis of fees to be charged,

So in addition to defining appropriate terms of reference, a consultant's proposal should quote:

- ▲ a fixed fee or
- ▲ a range within which the fee will fall or the fee rate(s) to be charged in terms of time (hour, day, week) or other defined basis.

WHAT TO DO ON APPOINTMENT

Draw up a contract with the consultants that states clearly and in detail the terms of the consultancy so that both sides know where they stand. The contract should include a copy of the agreed brief and/or the consultants' agreed proposal. Some consultants have their own standard contract, which should be read carefully and amended if necessary.

The contract should refer to:

- focus, aims and expectations of the work;
- how the work will be carried out, and what access to different parts of the organisation the consultants will need;
- to whom the consultants report;
  arrangements for reviewing work during the consultancy;
- professional responsibilities such as handling confidential information, avoiding conflicts of interest;
- fees to be paid and on what basis;
- expenses to be covered and arrangement for agreeing them;
- billing and payment arrangements;
- period of time contracted for – agree a timescale with 'milestones' for completion of specific aspects of the

MANAGING CONSULTANCY

　　　　work and for interim assessment – consider whether to include a time penalty in the contract;
- how the recommendations will be reported;
- agreement that a draft of any report will be shown to the person or committee commissioning the consultants to check for accuracy before any wider distribution within the organisation;
- whether there will be any follow-up meetings after the consultants have submitted their report.

Inform everyone in the organisation who has been contracted to do the work, what the timetable is, and which person or group is the main contact for the consultants.

Provide all the information requested by the consultants. Make sure you can offer the consultants the equipment and space for doing the work – such as a room or desk, phone, private meeting place for interviews, flip charts.

MANAGING THE CONSULTANCY

The key thing to remember is that this is your consultancy. So you must remain in control of it - retain 'ownership' of it and the issue being investigated. You must ensure that the consultancy is proceeding in the ways you want it to, and be in close contact with the consultants throughout the regular feedback sessions. This not only helps you to know what is going on but also enables problems to be raised and dealt with quickly. You should also keep the organisation as a whole in touch with how the work is going, whether it is as a director or management committee/board reporting back or through a special contact-person or steering group.

You should expect from the consultants:

- regular, jargon-free discussions about the work,
- efficiency and reliability,
- confidentiality,
- sensitivity to the demands made on staff by their regular work and by the consultants' own presence and questioning.

The consultants should expect from you:

- facts and information as required speedily and accurately,

full disclosure of all relevant information no matter how sensitive – don't worry, the consultants are bound to keep all information confidential both in the contract and according to their own profession's code of conduct (see The ethics of consultancy),
▶ co-operation across the organisation,
▶ immediate updating of major decisions taken by the organisation,
▶ the opportunity to talk in confidence with whom they wish within the organisation.

The level of importance attached to the consultants and the way they are treated – by management committee/board, director, senior staff, or any influential group of staff – will quickly be reflected in the overall attitude of the organisation to the consultancy. It is a significant event for an organisation, whether it be for a day or a year, and should be so regarded.

Even where there is serious disagreement within an organisation about the issues being investigated, or about having a consultancy 'imposed' on it, the consultants should be seen as a useful conduit for views and information – and valued as such.

WHEN THINGS GO WRONG

One recent survey[8] revealed that while 80% of consultancies were judged 'good' or 'excellent' by the commissioning organisations, one in five (20%) were disappointing to the organisations, with 11% of those considered to be 'poor'. This suggests that while you should certainly expect your consultancy to work well, you need to be prepared for and to guard against the possibility of something going wrong.

Problems can occur while the consultancy is going on or at the report stage. Whenever it happens, you need to be prepared. You can build into your regular meetings with the consultants a specific review of where things are going well and where they are not; or establish an unwritten agreement that allows for either side to say things are going wrong and to call a meeting to discuss the issues. Some organisations build a series of get-out and extension clauses into the original contract with the consultants to allow for unexpected happenings. It may be comforting to know that most such organisations report the clauses for extending a consultancy because it is proving so useful are invoked more often than the get-out clauses.

For guidance when something does go wrong, contact the Arts Council Marketing Unit, the Management Unit at the National Council for Voluntary Organisations, or – if relevant – the organisation that is funding your consultancy. If matters turn very unpleasant, contact the professional body to which your consultants belong (see Where to find out more for addresses and phone numbers) – and your own lawyers.

THE ETHICS OF CONSULTANCY

The professional bodies representing the consultancy industry have devised codes of professional conduct or ethics for their members. They largely focus on what is considered a proper standard of service to a client; what kind of working and financial agreements should be reached between consultants and clients; issues of confidentiality, independence, objectivity and integrity; plus upholding the good name of consultants.

These are all much the same, differing mainly in the level of detail. One difference is in recommendations for the financial arrangements for consultancy work (see Timing and cost).

These provide a useful framework within which to gauge how well your consultants are behaving towards you and what you should expect whether or not they are members of such bodies. By no means all are members, and this should not go against employing them.

One of the most comprehensive codes is produced by the Institute of Management Consultants (Fifth floor, 32/33 Hatton Garden, London EC1N 8DL; phone 071 242 2140). It includes such principles for members' behaviour as:

> 'A member will develop recommendations specifically for the solution of each client's problems; such solutions shall be realistic and practicable and clearly understandable by the client.'

and

> 'A member will not indicate any short-term benefits at the expense of the long-term welfare of the client, without advising the client of the implications.'

Confidentiality is a crucial element in the client-consultant relationship. It works both ways. Consultants should be expected to preserve your confidentiality. In turn, consultants will often want to keep conversations that they have within your organisation confidential.

RECEIVING THE RESULTS

Discuss well in advance how you want the consultants to report. This depends in part on the type of consultancy underway. For example, a feasibility study into new sources of funding should include a written report. But results of a consultancy on staff development are likely to be manifest in the increased performance and morale of the staff, or in the successful transfer to them of specific new skills.

The format for reporting should also square with how your organisation likes to deal with such material. Many organisations feel that they will only be getting value for money if they do receive a detailed, written report. But the 'report' can be in whatever forms are most useful to the organisation. The options include:

▶ a detailed written report;
▶ a short bullet-points report with presentation meeting by consultants;
▶ audio-visual presentation.

Decide also how the report and its recommendations are to be distributed internally. For example:

> who sees the full report;

MANAGING CONSULTANCY

- ▶ whether the consultants should give presentations to the staff, and what type of presentation would be most informative;
- ▶ what arrangements should be made for staff to meet to discuss the recommendations together and/or in groups.

Before any report, in whatever form, is made available to the organisation as a whole, it should be checked for accuracy. A report with valuable recommendations can lose credibility if it contains errors of fact, no matter how minor, especially if the consultancy has not had everyone's support.

With some types of consultancy, there is sometimes no specific end-result, merely discussions or ongoing adjustments to the way an organisation is operating, or a series of intermittent visits by consultants in an advisory capacity as and when the organisation requires that kind of additional input.

ASSESSING THE OUTCOME

The key questions are:

- have you got what you asked for?
- in the form you asked for?
- and, is it of value to the organisation – in effect, are you happy with it?

Other questions to bear in mind when evaluating a report include:

- is a solution offered?
- is the advice clear and coherent?
- have all the options been assessed?
- are the assumptions made about the organisation's situation and culture correct?
- are the implications of each option set out and
- assessed in human, financial or organisational terms?
- is all the relevant data set out? If not whose fault is it – the consultants for ignoring it or the organisation for not providing it when asked?

If you have kept in close touch with the consultants, then there should be few or no surprises. The report is merely consolidating what has already been flagged up by or even discussed in detail with the consultants. You can now move on to the implementation stage (see page xx).

However, sometimes matters do not go so well. For example, some voluntary and arts organisations have found that, come the final report, the consultants have based recommendations on misconceptions about the organisation, or offered solutions that do not square with the organisation's culture, aspirations or abilities. Such misreading of an organisation usually has its roots in inadequate liaison during the work, a failure to get across essential features of the organisation, or a belief by the consultants that the 'unacceptable' solution is the only effective way forward.

Whether such 'shock' tactics are deliberate or lack of foresight by consultants, the result is often justifiable resentment. One arts organisation director said that he was still dealing with the fall-out of a shock recommendation one year after the report was submitted. 'I wished for more insight into what the fall-out would be.'

Another consequence is that other, more acceptable recommendations can lose credibility if it is felt the consultants have misread the organisation.

So what should you do if you are unhappy with the result?

▶ check that the brief has been fulfilled; if not, ask the consultants to review their report so that it completes the agreed task.
▶ ask the consultants to explain why they recommend something considered 'unacceptable'; have they left some more acceptable avenues unexplored? do they realise it doesn't match the organisation's culture or core-aims?

There can be two forms of 'unacceptable' recommendation – a political one and a philosophical one. The first is unacceptable because it causes dissent and disruption within the organisation – say, merging two departments – but may not harm the organisation's core-values. The problem is either that the organisation does not wish to do anything unpleasant, or it was badly presented by the consultants. It can also have a positive effect. The chair of one voluntary organisation management committee explaining how the right moves came out of a misconceived consultancy report said: The unpopular recommendations provoked anger and stress which forced the organisation to change faster than it intended to.'

The recommendation that is philosophically unacceptable is more serious – such as asking an arts group to start charging fees when its whole purpose is to provide free access; proposing a hierarchical management structure in a collective enterprise; or suggesting volunteers should be phased out in favour of fewer but full-time paid staff to make an organisation more efficient. It is not that such against-the-grain recommendations should not be made – indeed, the challenge can shake up a complacent organisation and cause it to re-affirm its values and enable a confident one coherently to dismiss them. But they should be set out as one of several options with the implications of each described.

AFTER THE CONSULTANCY

STARTING THE DEBATE

You will want a lively debate within the organisation about the consultants' recommendations. But you will also want to establish a timetable for the debate so that the approved recommendations can be implemented quickly and effectively.

IMPLEMENTING THE RECOMMENDATIONS

If the consultancy has been about recommending new ways of working or of generating income and so on, you may need help in implementing the approved recommendations. If implementation has not been part of the original brief and budget, some consultants will raise the question of further work at an advanced stage of the consultancy once the tasks of implementation have become clear. They may offer one or two meetings after the brief has been completed and the report delivered for no extra fee. However, any longer-term work on implementation would have to be paid for.

It is really a question of the organisation deciding:

▶ what do we want to do next?
▶ are we able to carry it out on our own?

A day-long session three months hence may be a useful arrangement to see how the organisation has been operating and to iron out any problems.

With more 'concrete' outcomes, such as a report to be implemented, some consultants make sure that an organisation fully understands the report and is in a position to implement it. The consultants may then offer a new proposal for guiding through that implementation. However, the point of a consultancy for an organisation is not dependence but developing the ability to manage its own affairs.

> 'The hallmark . . . of a good consultancy relationship is one where the issue of disengagement is discussed and reviewed from the very outset; the consultant should be active in encouraging you to maintain your responsibility for managing the situation and planning his or her exit from your life.'[9]

CHECKLIST FOR A CONSULTANCY

Preparing for the consultancy

- Discuss the proposed consultancy within the organisation and how people are likely to be involved in and affected by it.
- Make sure everyone is clear about what the consultancy is about, and the advantages of bringing in consultants, and what they are expected to do.

Decide:

- whether to set up a steering group,
- who will prepare and agree the brief,
- how to choose the consultants,
- who will be the main contact for the consultants,
- how the organisation will be kept in touch with the progress of the consultancy.

Preparing the initial brief

- Set out the organisation's overall aims or mission statement.
- Identify the issue/problem to be tackled.
- Suggest how the work could be carried out.

MANAGING CONSULTANCY

- ▶ Define the aims of the consultancy.
- ▶ Propose an initial budget and time-scale.

Finding consultants

- ▶ Decide on the method(s) of finding suitable consultants – by personal recommendation, seeking advice from consultant-watchers, by advertising.

Choosing the consultants

- ▶ Finalise arrangements for choosing the consultants for the job.
- ▶ Compile a criteria-checklist for shortlisting consultants.
- ▶ Give likely and/or interested consultants details of your organisation, why you are calling in the consultants, and a copy of your initial brief.
- ▶ Ask consultants to submit an initial proposal for the work.
- ▶ Check references given.
- ▶ Either arrange preliminary discussions with likely consultants, or interview in depth the *most* promising candidates.

At the interview

- ▶ Make sure you meet the person/people who will carry out the work or will be your principal contact with the consultancy firm.
- ▶ Discuss:
  who will do the work and how many people will be working on the job;
  consultants' relevant experience;
  the schedule for the job;
  arrangements for monitoring and reporting back;
  the fee and how it will be paid;
  the estimated costs involved;
  whether payments should be linked to completion of specific stages of the work.

CHECKLIST FOR A CONSULTANCY

After the interview

- ▶ Eliminate those not suitable.
- ▶ Compare strengths and weaknesses.
- ▶ Compare fees quoted and estimated timescales.
- ▶ Check all unclear points.
- ▶ Assess genuine enthusiasm, commitment, and sympathy to core-values.
- ▶ Balance advantages and disadvantages.
- ▶ Decide which consultants you like and with whom you get on well.

Agreeing the final brief

- ▶ Discuss your initial brief and the consultants' proposal with the chosen consultants and refine together into a final brief.
- ▶ Agree on the timescale for the consultancy, how fees and costs will be calculated and paid.

On appointment

- ▶ Draw up and sign a contract with the consultants.
- ▶ Inform everyone in the organisation about the consultants, the timetable for the work, and who is to be the main contact for the consultants.
- ▶ Make arrangements to provide the consultants with the information, equipment, and space they require.

Managing the consultancy

- ▶ Keep in close contact with the consultants.
- ▶ Have regular feedback sessions with them.
- ▶ Keep the organisation in touch with what is happening.
- ▶ Make sure arrangements for the organisation's involvement in the consultancy are working smoothly.

Receiving the results

- ▶ Decide how you want the consultants to report their recommendations or conclusions to you.
- ▶ Check any report for accuracy before making it generally available.
- ▶ Decide how the report and/or its recommendations are to be distributed within the organisation.

Assessing the outcome

- ▶ Consider if you have got what you asked for, in the form you wanted it, and its value to the organisation.
- ▶ Discuss the report with the consultants and negotiate amendments or additions where the report fails to meet the agreed brief.

After the consultancy

- ▶ Decide how the report will be debated within the organisation and how to implement approved recommendations.
- ▶ Decide if you want further advice or guidance from the consultants and on what financial basis that might be.

WHERE TO FIND OUT MORE

ORGANISATIONS
Voluntary sector

Councils for Voluntary Service - National Association
26 Bedford Square
London WC1B 3HU
phone 071 636 4066

London Voluntary Service Council (LVSC)
68 Chalton Street
London NW1 1JR
phone 071 388 0241

National Council for Voluntary Organisations (NCVO)
26 Bedford Square
London WC1B 3HU
phone 071 636 4066

Northern Ireland Council of Voluntary Action
127 Ormeau Road
Belfast BT7 1SH
phone 0232 321224

Scottish Council for Voluntary Organisations
18/19 Claremont Crescent
Edinburgh EH7 4HX
phone 031 556 3882

Wales Council for Voluntary Action
Llys Ifor
Heol Crescent
Caerffilli
Canol Morgannwg CF8 1XL
phone 0222 869224

Arts sector

Arts Council
105 Piccadilly
London W1V OAU
phone 071 629 9495

Arts Council of Northern Ireland
181a Stranmillis Road
Belfast BT9 5DU
phone 0232 381591

Business in the Arts (ABSA)
Nutmeg House
60 Gainsford Street
Butlers Wharf
London SE1 2NY
phone 071 378 8143

Scottish Arts Council
12 Manor Place
Edinburgh EH3 7DD
phone 031 226 6051

Welsh Arts Council
Holst House
Museum Place
Cardiff CF1 3NX
phone 0222 394711

Professional bodies

Chartered Institute of Marketing
Moor Hall
Cookham
Maidenhead
Berkshire SL6 9QH
phone 06285 24922

Institute of Charity Fundraising Managers
208 Market Towers
Nine Elms Lane
London SW8 5NQ
phone 071 627 3436

Institute of Management Consultants (IMC)
32-33 Hatton Garden
London EC1N 8DL
phone 071 242 1803

Management Consultancies Association (MCA)
11 West Halkin Street
London SW1X 8JL
phone 071 235 3897

PUBLICATIONS
General books on running organisation:

Care, diligence and skill: a handbook for the governing bodies of arts organisations (Scottish Arts Council, 1987)

Getting organised: a handbook for non-statutory organisations by Christine Holloway and Shirley Otto (Bedford Square Press, 1986)

Just about managing? by Sandy Adirondack (London Voluntary Service Council, 1989)

Understanding voluntary organisations by Charles Handy (Pelican, 1988)

Practical advice on choosing and working with consultants:

Choosing a management consultant by Susan Elizabeth (NCVO News, March 1989)

Guidance notes and standard form of agreement between charities and fundraising consultants (ICFM and NCVO, 1989)

How to choose and use a management consultant by Max James, Simon Cotter, Alastair Fairley and Adrian Payne (The Economist Publications, 1989)

Incentive funding: the first year by Mary Allen and Howard Webber (Arts Council, 1989)

Issues in consultancy: reports of a series of seminars (NCVO Management Unit, 1989)

Management consultants: who they are and how to deal with them (Labour Research Department, 78 Blackfriars Road, London SE1 8HF, 1988)

Managerial consulting skills: a practical guide by Charles J Margerison (Gower, 1988)

MANAGING CONSULTANCY

Selection and use of management consultants (National Audit Office, Buckingham Palace Road, London SW1W 9DP, 1989)

Working with a management advisor: a Prudential guide for arts managers (ABSA/Business in the Arts, 1989)

Working with the arts: a Prudential guide for arts advisors (ABSA/Business in the Arts, 1989)

REFERENCES

1. from *Consulting to management* by Larry Greiner and Robert Metzger, Prentice-Hall, 1983.

2. from *Incentive funding: the first year,* Arts Council, October 1989.

3. from *Selection and use of management consultants,* National Audit Office, May 1989

4. from *The selection and use of management development consultants,* Local Government Training Board, 1984.

5. from *The selection and use of management development consultants,* Local Government Training Board, 1984.

6. from *Getting organised* by Christine Holloway and Shirley Otto (Bedford Square Press/NCVO, 1985).

7. *The Economist,* 13 February 1988.

8. from *Guidelines on charging for management consulting services,* Institute of Management Consultants, March 1983.

9. from *How to choose and use a management consultant,* The Economist Publications, April 1989.

10. from *The selection and use of management development consultants,* Local Government Training Board, 1984.